THE INFLUENCE OF MARITIME THEORISTS ON THE DEVELOPMENT OF
GERMAN NAVAL STRATEGY FROM 1930 TO 1936

A thesis presented to the Faculty of the U.S. Army
Command and General Staff College in partial
fulfillment of the requirements for the
degree

MASTER OF MILITARY ART AND SCIENCE
Strategy

by

Donald A. Cribbs, LCDR, USN
B.S. Physics, Virginia Military Institute, Lexington, VA, 1991

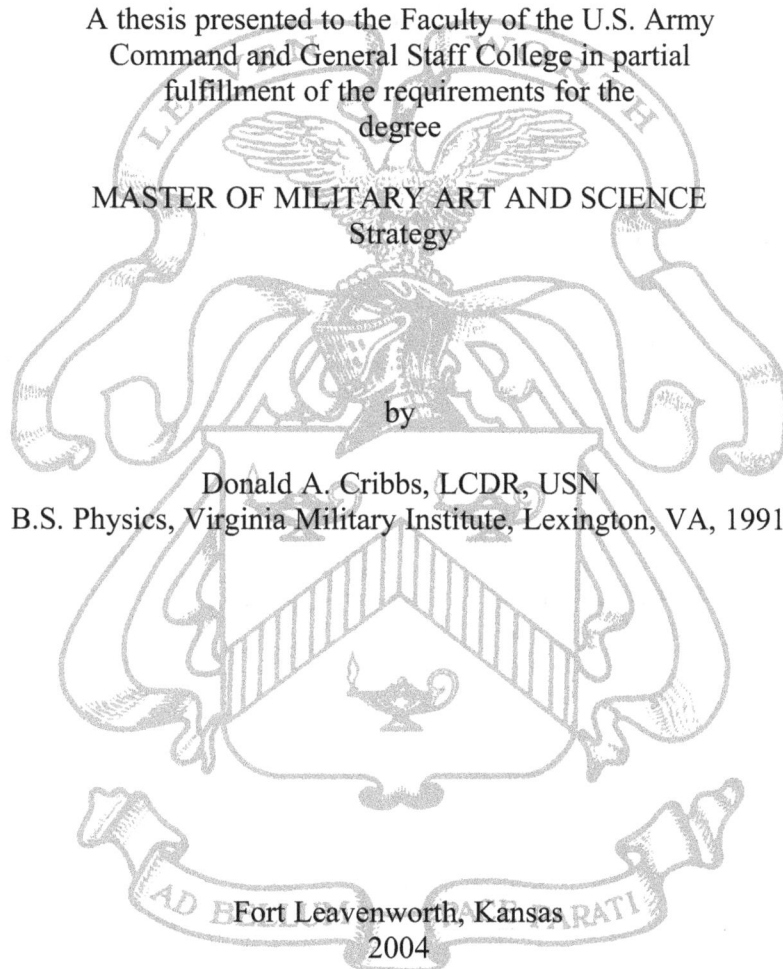

Fort Leavenworth, Kansas
2004

MASTER OF MILITARY ART AND SCIENCE

THESIS APPROVAL PAGE

Name of Candidate: LCDR Donald A. Cribbs

Thesis Title: The Influence of Maritime Theorists on the Development of German Naval Strategy from 1930 to 1936

Approved by:

_____, Thesis Committee Chair
CDR John T. Kuehn, M.M.A.S.

_____, Member
LTC Edward L. Bowie, M.M.A.S.

_____, Consulting Faculty
COL Kendra K. Kattelmann, Ph.D.

Accepted this 18th day of June 2004 by:

_____, Director, Graduate Degree Programs
Robert F. Baumann, Ph.D.

The opinions and conclusions expressed herein are those of the student author and do not necessarily represent the views of the U.S. Army Command and General Staff College or any other governmental agency. (References to this study should include the foregoing statement.)

Report Documentation Page

Form Approved
OMB No. 0704-0188

Public reporting burden for the collection of information is estimated to average 1 hour per response, including the time for reviewing instructions, searching existing data sources, gathering and maintaining the data needed, and completing and reviewing the collection of information. Send comments regarding this burden estimate or any other aspect of this collection of information, including suggestions for reducing this burden, to Washington Headquarters Services, Directorate for Information Operations and Reports, 1215 Jefferson Davis Highway, Suite 1204, Arlington VA 22202-4302. Respondents should be aware that notwithstanding any other provision of law, no person shall be subject to a penalty for failing to comply with a collection of information if it does not display a currently valid OMB control number.

1. REPORT DATE **17 JUN 2004**	2. REPORT TYPE	3. DATES COVERED **-**

4. TITLE AND SUBTITLE	5a. CONTRACT NUMBER
Influence of maritime theorists on the development of German naval strategy from 1930-1936	5b. GRANT NUMBER
	5c. PROGRAM ELEMENT NUMBER
6. AUTHOR(S) **Donald Cribbs**	5d. PROJECT NUMBER
	5e. TASK NUMBER
	5f. WORK UNIT NUMBER

7. PERFORMING ORGANIZATION NAME(S) AND ADDRESS(ES) **US Army Command and General Staff College,1 Reynolds Ave,Fort Leavenworth,KS,66027-1352**	8. PERFORMING ORGANIZATION REPORT NUMBER **ATZL-SWD-GD**

9. SPONSORING/MONITORING AGENCY NAME(S) AND ADDRESS(ES)	10. SPONSOR/MONITOR'S ACRONYM(S)
	11. SPONSOR/MONITOR'S REPORT NUMBER(S)

12. DISTRIBUTION/AVAILABILITY STATEMENT

Approved for public release; distribution unlimited

13. SUPPLEMENTARY NOTES

14. ABSTRACT

At the end of World War I, and upon the signing of the Treaty of Versailles, the German Armed Forces had been drastically reduced by the Allies. The German Navy was stripped of its battleships, submarines, and aircraft. The effort to rebuild began immediately following the war. The decision about what direction and shape the Navy would take was influenced by several factors. The German NavyŸs anticipated enemy, the restrictions of the Treaty of Versailles, and the political situation all played a part in the development of the post-World War I German Navy. At least as important as any of these factors was the influence of two prominent naval theorists, A.T. Mahan, and Sir Julian Corbett. This thesis examined the extent that the theories of Mahan and Corbett influenced the development of German Naval Strategy between 1930 and 1936. The period includes the remnants of the Weimar Republic, the ascension of Adolf Hitler, and the signing of the Anglo-German Naval agreement in 1935, and finally the first of naval developments after the treaty.

15. SUBJECT TERMS

16. SECURITY CLASSIFICATION OF:			17. LIMITATION OF ABSTRACT	18. NUMBER OF PAGES	19a. NAME OF RESPONSIBLE PERSON
a. REPORT **unclassified**	b. ABSTRACT **unclassified**	c. THIS PAGE **unclassified**	**1**	**67**	

Standard Form 298 (Rev. 8-98)
Prescribed by ANSI Std Z39-18

ABSTRACT

The Influence of Maritime Theorists on the Development of German Naval Strategy from 1930 to 1936, by LCDR Donald A. Cribbs

At the end of World War I, and upon the signing of the Treaty of Versailles, the German Armed Forces had been drastically reduced by the Allies. The German Navy was stripped of its battleships, submarines, and aircraft. The effort to rebuild began immediately following the war. The decision about what direction and shape the Navy would take was influenced by several factors. The German Navy's anticipated enemy, the restrictions of the Treaty of Versailles, and the political situation all played a part in the development of the post-World War I German Navy. At least as important as any of these factors was the influence of two prominent naval theorists, A.T. Mahan, and Sir Julian Corbett.

This thesis examined the extent that the theories of Mahan and Corbett influenced the development of German Naval Strategy between 1930 and 1936. The period includes the remnants of the Weimar Republic, the ascension of Adolf Hitler, and the signing of the Anglo-German Naval agreement in 1935, and finally the first of naval developments after the treaty.

ACKNOWLEDGMENTS

I owe a great many people a great deal thanks for their assistance in this effort.

CDR John Kuehn, USN, who served as my committee chairman for this project was an invaluable source of insight and endured countless questions from me. LTC Edward Bowie provided guidance and a unique perspective as an Army officer looking at naval matters. COL Kendra Kattlemann's willingness to serve as the committee's Ph.D. was greatly appreciated.

I would like to express my gratitude to Fregattenkapitaen Herbert Kraus and Dr Peter Popp of the Militaergeschichtliches Forschungsamt (Military History Research Bureau). Their assistance in providing research material for this project and assistance with clarifying some of my translations was critical.

Finally, I would like to thank my wife, Rebekah, who carried our first child through the time I spent working on this project. Her patience was truly a blessing.

TABLE OF CONTENTS

Page

CHAPTER 1

INTRODUCTION

After the final defeat of the Armed Forces of Imperial Germany in 1918, the new government and leadership of the remnants of the military had a monumental task. After not only a significant military defeat, but also under the strict constraints of the Treaty of Versailles, they had to redefine the strategy that would guide the new German Armed Forces, and find a way to rebuild their armed forces. The main question of this thesis is how did German naval strategy from 1930 to 1936 reflect the ideas of naval theorists?

Secondary Questions

The question of whether or not the German Navy developed an adequate strategy from 1930 to 1936 leads to several other questions, which will help to answer the main question.

One of the most important tasks for the navy was to define who its potential adversaries would be. The answer to that question would determine what kinds of forces were required, what missions they would be required to execute, and where the navy would have to operate. This would further determine the direction of research and development, and expenditure of national resources. Upon making a determination of who its prospective enemies might be, the allocation of national resources would become critical in defining the size of the navy that the economy and industrial base could support.

Very closely related to the determination of who the navy's future opponents might be was the issue of the navy's own strategic objectives. In order to develop a strategy, the navy would first have had to envision a realistic set of goals that it would be able to achieve within the framework of the purpose as set forth by the government. If the government decided that the navy would serve as a coastal defense force, then there would be no reason to plan for, or develop, an open ocean capability. So, the next question would be whether or not the navy pursued those technological advances that would have given them the capabilities they needed to fulfill the government's purpose. Also, the navy would have needed to be prepared to participate in international agreements and treaties that could impact its size and capabilities. For example, what preparations did the navy make prior to the signing of the Anglo-German Naval Agreement of 1935?

Also, to what extent did the navy attempt to influence the government's formulation of a national strategic vision? If the navy remained completely passive while the government was developing a post-war strategic policy, then they could very well have been marginalized, or tasked to carry out entirely unrealistic missions. However, by using some measure of influence, the navy would have been able to have a say in the organization that determined their fate.

Definitions

Strategy is defined as the plan for an organization to achieve a set of goals. In this case, it refers to the long-range plan developed by the leadership of the navy to achieve military success with the framework of the overall national strategy developed by the German government.

The leadership of the German navy is defined as those individuals, military and civilian, who had the ability to define and influence the navy's long-term strategic goals.

OKW (Oberkommando der Wehrmacht). The High Command of the Armed Forces was the equivalent of the Joint Chiefs of Staff in the United States. However, there was no equivalent of the Combatant Commanders in the German Armed Forces of that time. Operations were conducted by the various service elements.

OKM (Oberkommando der Marine. Prior to 1935, it was known as Die Marineleitung). The Supreme Naval Command does not have an equivalent in the modern US Navy. The OKM was responsible for administrative and operational matters.

Ob.d.M (Oberbefehlshaber der Marine. Prior to 1935, this position was known as "Chef der Marineleitung"). The Supreme Commander in Chief of the Navy. The Ob.d.M was the senior officer in the navy. This position would be roughly equivalent to the current position in the United States Navy of Chief of Naval Operations (CNO). However, the CNO in the modern US Navy does not have any operational authority. The Ob.d.M was responsible for the conduct of all naval operations approved by the OKW. From 1928 to 1943, the Ob.d.M was Admiral Raeder, who was tried and convicted at the Nuremberg Trials.

Kaiserliche Marine. The Imperial Navy's name from its inception in 1871 under Kaiser Wilhelm I until it was disbanded at the end of the First World War.

Reichsmarine. The best translation in contemporary language would be the Imperial navy. Because the Kaiser was deposed at the end of the First World War, a new name was needed for the navy, which reflected the change in government in post-war Germany. Reichsmarine was used from 1920 to 1935.

Kriegsmarine. The best translation for this title would be "War Navy." The Reichsmarine was renamed this in 1935 when the German Armed Forces were officially reestablished.

Limitations

This paper is limited to topics relating to the development of an overall maritime strategy by the German Navy. The overarching national strategy put into effect by Hitler as the leader of the German National Socialist Workers Party (National Sozialistische Deutsche Arbeiter Partei, NSDAP) certainly had a massive impact on how the navy decided upon a strategy. However, the goals and policies of the NSDAP will be discussed only as they relate to the navy. Also, Hitler's military strategy is only relevant as it applied to the Navy for this paper.

Furthermore, this paper will only address the merits and demerits of various weapons systems as they apply at the strategic level. There are a great many sources of information on the exact capabilities of the different submarines and surface ships. A detailed discussion of this subject is outside the scope of this paper.

A further limitation is the availability of first hand research material. The German Navy kept extensive records throughout its existence. However, these records are in the original German, and currently reside in the German Military Archives in Freiburg. The amount of time for research does not lend itself to an extensive investigation of inter-war documents.

This thesis will address the primary question in four major parts. First, the primary maritime theorists of the day will be analyzed, so that their views can be applied to the actions of the German navy. Also, other pertinent literature concerning the history of Germany and the German navy will be examined to provider a broader view of the subject. Then, the development of strategy of the German Navy from its inception to 1929 will be discussed to provide a historical background for the time period of this thesis, and to discuss the genesis of German naval strategy up to that point. Next, the strategy adopted by the German Navy from 1930 to 1936 will be analyzed in an attempt to answer the main question of this thesis. The period from 1930 to 1936 was chosen because it included the last German government before the rise of the NDSAP, the rise of Hitler, the Anglo-German Naval Agreement of 1935, and the repercussions of that agreement in 1936. These factors are important because they represent a period of great political change and a period of change in naval strategy. Finally, the conclusions from the answer to the main question will be discussed in the final chapter.

CHAPTER 2

LITERATURE REVIEW

In attempting to determine the strategic basis was for the development of the

German Navy, the first step must be to understand the strategic theories of maritime

power that existed during the interwar period. Admiral Alfred Thayer Mahan and Sir

Julian Corbett developed differing, but very insightful theories about seapower. Theirs

were the pre-eminent theories concerning the meaning, development, and execution of

seapower. An understanding of these theories will provide the framework for answering

the main question of this thesis.

Mahan

Alfred Thayer Mahan was an officer in the United States Navy. He was

commissioned in 1859, and served in the vessels conducting the blockade of the

Confederacy during the Civil War. However, he did not experience combat during the

war. After the Civil War, he held a series of relatively nondescript assignments, until

1886, when he was assigned to the newly created Naval War College, where he was to

teach tactics and history. [1] Four years after reporting the War College, he published *The

Influence of Seapower Upon History*. Mahan's book was an instant success, and

generated profound interest throughout the world. He was received by senior officials in

both imperial Japan and the United Kingdom. He later published several other books and

articles, all concerning seapower.

Mahan believed that historians had largely ignored the role that seapower played

in history. Mahan's book outlined the European naval conflicts between France, Spain, the Netherlands, and Great Britain up through the American Revolutionary War period. In these examples, he saw that seapower had played a critical role that had a significant impact in the overall campaigns, but had received little recognition from historians.[2]

Furthermore, Mahan defined "six principle conditions" which affect a nation's seapower. They were geographical position, physical conformation, extent of territory, number of population, character of the people, and the character of the government.[3]

The geographic position of a nation has a most significant impact on the development of that nation's seapower. Obviously, a landlocked nation may be concerned with the economic benefits that may come from the ocean, and from oceanographic exploration, however, they will not be concerned with developing a navy.[4] A non-island nation, especially one with hostile neighbors will be required to maintain an army to defend it. Coastlines have proven to be avenues for invading armies throughout history, as well as international borders. England has always been able to focus her efforts and resources on seapower for the simple fact of being an island nation. However, France and the Netherlands struggled to maintain a balance between having a naval fleet, and armies.[5]

The position of a nation in relation with respect to other nations, and with respect to the geographic features around it plays a very significant role in the development of seapower. England has been given a significant natural advantage in being on the northern side of the English Channel, and the western side of the North Sea. From this position England has the ability to affect all of the maritime traffic coming from the Baltic, and from the Netherlands, Belgium, Germany, and the Scandinavian countries. Not only by the virtue of its own position, but also by the location of its colonies, may a nation have the ability to exert tremendous influence at sea. Again, England provides an excellent example. Gibraltar and Malta give England the ability to monitor, and when necessary, provide a base of operations in the Mediterranean.[6]

A combination of the previously listed characteristics is that of "commerce-destroying," as it was known in Mahan's time.[7] A nation's ability to project seapower based on its location and that of its colonies gives it the ability to conduct commerce-destroying. Mahan believed that the ability to intercept, and capture or destroy an enemies merchant fleet was greatly a function of its geographic position. The principle of commerce raiding will appear again.

The second factor that affects a nation's sea power is physical conformation. If a nation has an extensive coastline, but few ports which are capable of supporting large ships, then that nation is at a disadvantage. However, again using England as an example, an abundance of deepwater ports permits the development of several locations for the use of on, and offloading cargo, and for the location of shipyards. On the southern coast alone, England boasts such excellent harbors as Plymouth, Portsmouth, and Dover. In addition to these, England has several ports along their western border on the Irish Sea, and along the North Sea. If the ports in Scotland are considered as well, then England clearly has the benefit of a coastline conducive the development of seapower. These ports give the English an advantage over the French, who have, at best, five harbors along their entire Atlantic seaboard.[8]

Another factor of a nation's physical conformation is the abundance, or lack thereof, of estuaries. Rivers provide natural "highways" which facilitate commerce from the internal areas of a country to its ports. A large number of rivers allows for the involvement of a greater portion of a nation in the economic growth that comes with the increased trading opportunities fostered by maritime trade. In war, rivers provide the means for naval forces to withdraw into a protected area. Mahan's example of Germany illustrates how rivers can be used to carry trade from regions of a nation distant from the coast to its harbors.[9]

Extent of territory is the next subject that Mahan chooses to address. The length of the coastline which a nation must defend can either provide an advantage, or disadvantage, based on the nature of the people of that nation and its population, as will be discussed later. Mahan used the example of the Confederacy during the American Civil War to show that an extensive coastline with numerous rivers providing access to the interior became a liability for the South due to their relatively low population, and the fact that they were not a seagoing culture.[10]

As mentioned above, the number of a population is a factor which Mahan addresses as a factor in a nation's ability to develop sea power. The larger the part of a nation's population which may be called into maritime service yields an increased amount of seapower which that nation may develop. Although it would seem that the number of people involved in maritime related endeavors in peacetime would yield a greater number of personnel going to sea in naval vessels in times of crisis, this is not necessarily the case. Sir Edward Pellew, an English naval officer, was faced with a lack of seamen when war broke with France in the late 18th century. In 1793, he instructed his officers to look for Cornish miners, as the dangerous nature of the work would make them ideal for sea duty. Despite the unorthodox nature of his recruiting efforts, he defeated an enemy frigate in his first engagement after leaving port.[11] Mahan further

9

states that it is not only the number of men available during times of peace, but the ability of a reserve to go to sea at the outset of hostilities. So, the size of the sea-going population of a nation is a factor in its ability to develop seapower.

Not only does the size of a nation's population affect its seapower, but also the character of its population. An interest and desire to explore, travel, and trade with distant nations are all characteristics of a populace interested in maritime affairs. This provides the base for both commercial and naval fleets. Mahan brings up another aspect of the characteristic of a population. He contrasts Spain and Portugal with England and the Netherlands. According to Mahan, Spain and Portugal became wealthy because of the materials that their merchant fleets brought from their colonies in the new world. The gold and silver that came from the mines of Central and South America created great wealth for the two nations; however, they did create a growing domestic economy to further develop their nation's economic strength. Rather, they became dependant on their imports. England and the Netherlands, on the other hand, used their merchant fleets to trade with other nations, and to export what they produced. This fostered the development of industry which proved to outlast the imported wealth of Spain and Portugal. The character of the nations proved to be as important to their developing seapower as any of the other factors. [12]

Finally, Mahan addresses the character of the government as the last of the six issues that affect a nation's ability to develop sea power. A government with the vision and determination to develop sea power, especially when combined with the will of the people, has the potential to become a maritime power. When the government has the vision to build ships, especially when they are willing to accept risk and strive for innovation, and has the foresight to recruit its citizens as seamen, and create conditions

which will encourage them to remain in service, will certainly lead its people to

prominence at sea. In summary, Mahan believed a nation's seapower was a function of

both its maritime commerce and its navy. In war, he saw decisive fleet engagements as

the key to gaining the advantage over a maritime enemy. [13]

Mahan wrote many books that discussed other aspects of maritime warfare. For

example, he wrote about the composition of a fleet and what kind of ships it should

consist of.

> Whether to build a navy of "a few very big ships, or more numerous medium
> ships might be arguable . . . the maximum power of the fleet . . . and not the
> maximum power of the single ship is the true object of battleship construction." [14]

Written before the development of naval aviation, this view reflected the primary

importance of the battleship. However, his statement that "the maximum power of the

fleet" was most important illustrated that he was thinking beyond ship type. Had he

written this article forty years later, he would have undoubtedly included the aircraft

carrier due the striking power it added to fleets.

Mahan discussed other subjects as well. Not only was the composition of a fleet a

subject of interest for him, but the employment of a fleet was a subject he wrote about.

He said that the single result of all naval action was the destruction of the enemy's

organized force and the establishment of one's own control of the sea. [15] He developed a

vision of a decisive engagement between two fleets, with the victor being able to

establish control of the sea and from that achieve victory over one's enemies.

Corbett

Sir Julian Stafford Corbett was born in London in 1854. The son of a well-to-do architect, he read law at Trinity College, and achieved first class honors. He became a barrister in 1877, but did not work full time due to his independent wealth. He traveled, and in 1886 published the first of several novels. They made little money, and in 1898, he published his first historical book, a two-volume work titled *Drake and the Tudor Navy*. It was much more successful than any of his novels, and in 1899, he decided to devote all of his efforts to naval historiography. In 1902, Corbett was invited to the Royal Naval College to begin lecturing. This began his association with the Royal Navy which was to last, in varying degrees for the rest of his life. Many of the theories he advanced were very controversial, but he always found supporters, within and without, the Royal Navy.[16] One of his most important supporters was Admiral Fischer, future First Sea Lord of the Royal Navy, and father of the Dreadnought class battleship.

Corbett's crowning achievement was *Some Principles of Maritime Strategy*. Published in 1911, it received immediate attention, both positive and negative. Some of his theories were contrary to those of Mahan, who was widely regarded as a, if not the, leading expert on Naval Strategy. *Some Principles of Maritime Strategy* represented the collective thoughts that Corbett had been working on during his tenure at the Royal Naval College. He takes a different direction in developing his ideas on maritime strategy in that he discusses outright strategic principles, compared to Mahan's use of historical examples to discuss the influence of seapower.

In the first chapter, Corbett states that the central theme to his book is maritime, vice naval. He contends that "it is almost impossible for a war to be decided by naval action alone."[17] Another of his main points in the first chapter is to make the point that it is necessary to emphasize the interdependence of land and sea aspects of war. Also, Corbett makes extensive reference, and comparison, to Clausewitz. He compares and contrasts the maritime theory of war to the overall theory of war. He describes the differences between war on land and war at sea, yet realizes that Clausewitz's overarching theories apply as much to maritime warfare as to land warfare. Specifically, he states that war is a means of political action, and also, discusses limited versus unlimited war. Corbett makes his most fundamental statement in Chapter Three when he says that: "The object of naval warfare must always be directly or indirectly either to secure the command of the sea or to prevent the enemy from securing it."[18] He then goes on to define command of the seas as "nothing but the control of maritime communications, whether for commercial or military purposes."[19] Corbett then goes on to further define maritime communications, the role of the "cruiser," the role and practice of commerce destroying, and many other topics pertinent to the discussion of maritime strategy.

Corbett continued to develop the connection between the effectiveness of command of the sea with the effectiveness of a nation's ability to wage war. He stated that

> Consequently by denying an enemy this means of passage we check the movement of his national life at sea in the same kind of way we check it on land by occupying his territory.[20]

Corbett saw the benefit in using naval forces to deny a nation the use of the seas as a means of moving materials vital to that nation's economy. By choking off these materials, naval forces could have a significant impact on the conduct of a campaign ashore.

In summary, Corbett believed that the main focus of naval warfare was command of the sea. He then went on to define command of the sea as control of maritime communications. The importance of controlling maritime communications was to have the ability to protect one's own maritime commerce, and prevents the adversary from using the seas for communications.

Biographies

Although the records of the OKM, and other naval organizations of the interwar period remain overseas, there are two notable firsthand accounts available to the public. Admirals Raeder and Doenitz both published memoirs after their imprisonment. They were certainly the principle authors of the maritime strategy in the interwar period. Rader was responsible for the overall naval strategy and Doenitz developed the strategy for the submarine force. Their experiences are useful sources of firsthand information regarding German Naval strategy. However, it is very important to realize that both men were convicted by the war crimes court at Nuremberg. Raeder and Doenitz both used their memoirs as vehicles to excuse and explain their roles in the Second World War. Many well-known historical facts, such as their personal disagreements with each other, were completely ignored. [21] In fact, rather than acknowledge this very public disagreement, Raeder washes it over by saying that the selection of then Junior Captain Karl Doenitz, as head of the submarine force "without shadow of doubt, was right."[22] Further, Raeder devotes an entire chapter in his dedication to upholding the church's influence in the Navy. In his biography, *Ten Years and Twenty Days*, Doenitz also paints a completely

14

rosy picture of his relationship with Raeder, and, of course, denies any knowledge of the atrocities committed by Germans under the Nazi regime. Although both men were principle authors of the German Naval Strategy in the interwar period, the works they published after the war are very colored by their efforts to explain, and excuse their actions.

War Records

Written records of the meetings, papers, and other documents are a useful group of sources available to the researcher interested in the development of naval strategy. The German Armed Forces had a penchant for saving all of their printed documents. At the end of the war, these records were discovered in a hidden cavern in the Hartz Mountains. The records were confiscated by the Allies and eventually found their way to the Royal Archives in the United Kingdom and United States. They were eventually returned to Germany, where they are now kept in Freiburg. Because the records were interned in the United States, and United Kingdom, German historians did not have a chance to examine the records, and begin analyzing the contents until their return.[23] German historians, such as Michael Salewski, Jost Duelffer, and Gerhart Schreiber have all published works regarding the German Navy between wars using these documents.[24]

Translations

Appendices A and B are translation by the author of two articles by a prominent German naval historian, Dr. Werner Rahn. Dr Rahn has published several other articles relating to the history of the German Navy and is a retired German naval officer who was the director of the Military History Research Institute of the German Armed Forces in

Potsdam. The sections of the articles translated in the appendices are of particular interest because they reveal the state of the German Government and the German Navy immediately after the First World War. In this environment the future existence of the German Navy hung in the balance. Struggling to ensure its survival, the formulation of a long-term strategy was of secondary importance.

Conclusion

The works of the principle theoreticians of maritime strategy in the interwar period provide an excellent baseline for evaluating maritime strategies developed in that era. Mahan and Corbett wrote detailed descriptions of their understanding of how the strategy of the sea had developed, and would most likely continue to develop. Their works offer a means of measuring the strategic reasoning for the development of the German Navy in the interwar period. Other materials provide further insights into the thoughts of the leadership of the German Navy; some are useful to provide factual information, others useful provided they are read with an understanding of the author's motives for writing them. All together, there is more than sufficient material available to effectively analyze the main question of this thesis.

---

[1] Alfred Thayer Mahan, *The Influence of Sea Power Upon History, 1660-1783* (New York: Hill and Wang, 1957), vi.

[2] Ibid., ix. Mahan also mentions Hannibal's campaign against the Romans, and the effect that Roman seapower had on the Carthaginians. Had Hannibal been able to transport his army via the sea to a location closer to Rome, and not lost a significant portion of his forces marching through the Alps, how would the outcome of the Punic Campaign been different?

[3] Ibid., 25.

[4]The Swiss do not have a navy, but do participate in research relating to the sea, such as in Antarctica, for example, and are certainly affected by maritime commerce, as in the transportation of petroleum.

[5]Mahan, 26

[6]Ibid., 29

[7]Ibid., 27

[8]Ibid., 29

[9]Ibid., 36

[10]Ibid., 38

[11]Ibid., 40

[12]Ibid., 46

[13]Ibid., 76

[14]Peter Paret, *Makers of Modern Strategy*, (Princeton, Princeton University Press, 1986). pp 458

[15]Ibid., 458

[16]Julian Stafford Corbett, *Some Principles of Maritime Strategy*, (Annapolis: Naval Institute Press, 1988), xxx

[17]Ibid., 15

[18]Ibid., 91

[19]Ibid., 94

[20]Corbett, 93.

[21]Anthony Mortenssen, *Hitler and His Admirals*, (New York: E. P. Dutton and CO., 1949), p. xx

[22]Erich Raeder, *Grand Admiral*, (Annapolis: US Naval Institute Press, 1960), page 172. In fact, Raeder makes no mention of his oft disparaging comments about Doenitz. This is certainly a reflection of the willingness to gloss over possibly adverse facts in order to present a positive public opinion.

[23]Charles Thomas, *The German Navy in the Nazi Era*, (Annapolis: Naval Institute Press, 1990), pp. xiii-xiv.

[24]Ibid., xiv

CHAPTER 3

THE FOUNDATIONS OF GERMAN NAVAL STRATEGY

Introduction

An understanding of the central question begins much earlier than 1930. In order to comprehend the strategies and policies of the period in question, a review of the events which led to their creation is necessary. The policies of Germany in the mid to late thirties were a direct product of the policies conducted at the inception of Germany as a nation. They are intertwined, and the outcome of the latter was determined by the execution of the former.

On 18 January 1871, Wilhelm I of Prussia was proclaimed Kaiser of a united Germany in the Hall of Mirrors in Versailles, France. This was a result of the Franco-Prussian War, where the military forces of not only Prussia, but the other German states defeated the French armies of Napoleon III. The part of Germany over which he was proclaimed emperor did not, at that time, include the southern states of Württemberg, and Bavaria. However, when faced with the prospects of being the only outsiders in a unified Germany, they quickly changed their minds. The architect of this unification was the Minister President of Prussia, Otto von Bismarck.

Bismarck was a minor aristocrat from the Prussian land owning class. He was originally opposed to parliamentary democracy; however, one of his great strengths was his ability to understand the political forces at work in a given situation. He realized in the early sixties that unification was Germany's future. Accordingly, he pursued those policies which would lead to Germany's unification. He was also skillful in the arena of strategic thinking. He realized that Germany would need to consider the effects of her actions on the rest of Europe. The fundamental lack of this ability is apparent several times in Germany's history, to include the period covered the central question of this thesis.

After the creation of a unified Germany, Bismarck continued to serve as Minister President under the new Kaiser Wilhelm I. Frederick III succeeded his father, but was diagnosed with throat cancer, and reined for only ninety days. He was succeeded by his son Wilhelm II. This began a period of change in Germany for two reasons. First, Wilhelm II began to have significant differences with Bismarck relatively early on. Second, Wilhelm II was a great admirer of the English. His father, Frederick III, married Queen Victoria's daughter. He felt a great affinity for the English and especially admired their navy and the power it brought them.

By early 1890, Bismarck had been ousted as Chancellor of Germany. The loss of the guiding influence, and source of strategic vision, for Germany's foreign policy had a significantly negative impact. Wilhelm II's admiration for the English, especially their navy, led him to attempt to duplicate some of the most important aspects of the Royal Navy. His pursuit had a most detrimental effect on Germany's standing with the rest of Europe.

Wilhelm II had always seen himself as a very military-minded ruler. However, he had never been in combat, and never had any formal military education. Count von Waldersee, Chief of the German General Staff observed:

> I am convinced that the monarch has a certain understanding of parade-ground movements, not, however, of real troop-leading. What is missing is an experience of war. . . . [He] is extraordinarily restless, dashes back and forth, is much too far forward in the fighting line, intervenes in the leadership of the generals, gives countless and often contradictory orders, and scarcely listens to his

advisors. He always wants to win, and when the decision of the judge is against him, takes it ill.[1]

Clearly, the military did not think highly of Wilhelm II. But a clear distinction must be made. The military up to the reign of Wilhelm II was very much the Army. The German Navy had languished in the shadow of the Army. The officers of the Army were very strongly represented by the landed aristocracy of the Prussian Junkers. The success of the Prussian Army had been the decisive factor in the establishment of a unified Germany, and the Navy had taken a much less significant position. When Wilhelm II ascended to the throne, this began to change.

As stated earlier, Wilhelm II had a deep admiration of all things English, including, and perhaps especially, their navy. When Mahan published his work, it had an immediate impact on the new king. Wilhelm II, influenced by his admiration for the Royal Navy and by Mahan's analysis of the importance of a navy, started down a policy path that would have the most serious of consequences for Germany and Europe. Wilhelm II decided to develop a German Navy that would rival the Royal Navy. Bismarck would almost certainly have recognized the folly in such a move, as the Royal Navy had always been the guarantor of England's security. However, with Bismarck gone, there was no one to prevent Wilhelm II from pursuing his goal of advancing Germany's prestige by building a world class navy, whether Germany needed one or not. Under the guidance of Admiral Tirpitz the German Navy started to grow in both size and significance. Tirpitz had served in the very small Prussian Navy during the Franco-Prussian War. During this time, the main supply base for the Prussian Navy had been at Plymouth, in England. This is almost certainly where Tirpitz had his first close contact with the Royal Navy. Tirpitz described the English as condescending, and this impression stayed with him.[2] After Germany's defeat of the French, the navy began to grow. However, it was not until the ascension of Wilhelm II, that the growth became significant.

Tirpitz first met the new king in 1887, when he commanded the torpedo squadron that accompanied Wilhelm II to England for Queen Victoria's jubilee.[3] Wilhelm II personally appointed Tirpitz as Chief of Staff to the Executive Command in 1892. This allowed Tirpitz to carry out many changes to the training and operations of the German Navy. Tirpitz's next assignment was as Chief of the Eastern Asiatic Cruiser Division, where he was directed to locate a future military base on the Chinese coast. He succeeded in finding a base, but his dealings further refined his previous impression, to the point where came to consider Great Britain as Germany's chief enemy.[4] The Kaiser did not share Tirpitz's view of England as Germany's main rival; however, their views on building a navy equivalent to England's were shared.

Therefore, in 1898, Tirpitz proposed a budget to support a naval construction plan that would yield nineteen battleships, eight coastal armored ships, twelve large, and thirty small cruisers, and a supporting force of torpedo boats, and support ships.[5] Furthermore, as a result of the Spanish-American War, he requested, in 1900, to double the number of battleships.[6] The supplemental budget was passed, and the ratio of German battleships to English went from two to one to three to two. Although many in England had not felt threatened by the original increase in the size of the German Navy, the passage of the supplemental budget caused much concern.[7] Germany was clearly on a path to a much larger navy than she had ever had before, but lacked anyone with the strategic vision of Bismarck to see the consequences.

Once the supplemental budget was passed, the influence of naval theorists became apparent. If Germany's goal was to build a navy that would be a counter-balance to the English navy, then building the largest fleet, the best fleet possible, would be their goal. This fleet, growing towards parity with the English fleet in number of battleships, would clearly have as its purpose a decisive engagement against the English grand fleet. In a memorandum to the king in 1897, Tirpitz made his position very clear:

> That German ships must be built to meet "the most difficult situation in war into which our fleet can come," and went on to say, "For Germany, the most dangerous enemy at the present time is England. It is also the enemy against which we most urgently require a certain measure of naval force as a political factor." Against an antagonist like England, commerce-raiding would be useless. "Our fleet must be constructed so that it can unfold its greatest military potential between Helgoland and the Thames . . . The military situation against England demands battleships in as great a number as possible."[8]

This is an entirely Mahanian vision of naval strategy. Had Germany wanted a means of strategically isolating England from the sea, then a fleet focused on commerce-raiding would have been sufficient. However, Tirpitz followed Mahan's theory of seeking a fleet on fleet confrontation at sea, and continued with his building plan.

In 1907, partially in response to the growing German navy, the Royal Navy introduced the Dreadnought class battleship, and changed the definition of the battleship. The Dreadnought was a large all big gun ship that could outrange and outmaneuver all previous classes of battleships. This obviously posed a significant problem for Tirpitz who had only a few years previously received funding to initiate a major building program for the German Navy. He was forced to request another supplement to the naval budget.[9] It was approved, and the naval buildup continued until the outbreak of the First World War.

A detailed description of the various activities of the German Navy during the First World War is beyond the scope of this thesis. However, there are a few points that are relevant to the central question and theme of this thesis. These are: the engagement of the vast fleets of large surface ships, fighting a decisive battle at sea, and the emergence of the submarine.

First, Tirpitz's purpose in building a large fleet of battleships was to be able to challenge to the Royal Navy at sea. Therefore, he envisioned that at some point in the war, the two fleets would come into direct contact en masse, and a decisive battle would occur, rendering one fleet the supreme victor, and relegating the other to the status of the defeated party for the remainder of the war. The German Navy launched several raids against the coast of England, however, they were short in nature, and did not bring them into contact with the main portion of the Royal Navy. There were two engagements in August 1914, and another in January 1915. These battles were not the large engagements envisioned by Tirpitz, and did not render the decision he wanted. The largest naval engagement of the war was the Battle of Jutland from May 31 to June 1, 1916. Admiral Scheer instituted a more aggressive policy than that of his predecessor, and, in an effort to engage the Royal Navy, sortied the majority of his fleet in search of their opponents. The British, who had intercepted, and de-crypted German signals, were aware of the German plan, and sailed to meet them. The ensuing battle would see the largest concentration of warships in history to that time; however, the outcome was far from decisive in the tactical sense. Strategically, the victory went to the British, as the German Navy never set sail again in such numbers; in fact the majority of the fleet remained in harbor for the rest of the war. The fleet that had consumed so much German capital and industrial resources had failed to meet the purpose for which it was created.[10]

In direct contrast to the large fleet of battleships built by the German Navy was the submarine fleet. The submarine was built with the intention of acting in support of major fleet operations. As indicated in the quote above, Tirpitz did not think much of commerce raiding, and felt that battleships were the key to the fleet. However, as proved by the earliest surface engagements and the Battle of Jutland, battleships would not necessarily render the decisive outcome he had hoped for. As early as late 1914, after the initial failure of surface vessels to achieve a decisive engagement against the Royal Navy, Tirpitz started to change his opinion about commerce raiding.

> Conveniently forgetting his pre-war scorn of commerce raiding and his advocacy of the doctrines of Alfred Thayer Mahan, Alfred von Tirpitz placed himself in the van of the new movement. In late November he granted an interview to the American journalist Karl von Wiegand, which was published on 22 December 1914, in which he announced a German submarine blockade that would close British waters to shipping. [11]

The rules of maritime warfare did not favor the submarine. Submarines were required to surface and search a merchant vessel prior to taking any action. If contraband was found, the submarine was then required to allow the crew and passengers to abandon ship, and ensure that they were safe.[12] A submarine on the surface is all but helpless against a surface vessel. As the war progressed, and Germany's situation became tenuous, the advocates of unrestricted warfare won out, and Germany resumed a policy of unrestricted submarine warfare. Although the campaign initially achieved impressive results, the British eventually adopted the convoy system, and the effectiveness of the submarine diminished significantly.[13] The most effective maritime weapon employed by the German Navy in the First World War was not the battleship, but the submarine. In spite of the emphasis on Mahan's theories of building the best navy affordable, and seeking a decisive engagement on the high seas, the most effective part of the maritime campaign against England was waged by the submarine fleet. The idea of raiding an enemy's commerce is much more in line with Corbett's theories than with Mahan's. It was at the end of the war that the German Navy began to diverge from its stated goals of adhering to Mahan's theories in favor of Corbett's.

The First World War ended in disaster for Germany. The Hohenzollern dynasty was forced into exile in the Netherlands, and the treaty of Versailles imposed drastic restrictions on Germany and her armed forces. As part of the terms of surrender, the ships of the German navy were to be interred in a neutral port. However, once the armistice was signed the allies directed the ships to Scappa Flow, a Royal Navy Base in Scotland. In a final act of defiance, the senior officer in charge of the interred fleet ordered the ships scuttled. This deprived the Allies of taking possession of the ships. The German Navy saw this as a means to preserve some measure of their honor. The Allies permitted Germany to retain a very limited number of ships and banned them from possessing submarines. The reaction to submarines was particularly noteworthy, as it was an expression of the reprehension felt by most of the world regarding the submarine campaign conducted by the Germans. The beginning of the 1920's found Germany with a miniscule fleet of older ships, a few minesweepers, support ships, and no submarines.

There was much political turmoil in Germany after the First World War. The revolution forced the royal family into exile, so a new republican government had to be created. The new government had briefly considered abolishing the German Navy. However, the action of several proponents of the German Navy, both military and civilian, kept the navy alive. They put forth a shipbuilding program to the extent that it was possible under the Treaty of Versailles, and feasible under the economic constraints of post war Germany. By the middle of the 1920's, Germany had initiated a covert arms research program with the goal of keeping up with advances in military technology forbidden to them by the Treaty of Versailles. Among the various military technologies being developed were patrol torpedo boats and submarines.[14] German naval engineers were positioned in every corner of Europe, from Sweden to Greece, and from Spain to Russia. Their efforts at furthering research and development into the weapons systems prohibited by the Treaty of Versailles were funded from secret government accounts. Sometimes the managers of these accounts were caught, and political scandal was the result. However, the research and technological development continued.

Not only was the German effort to develop military technology noteworthy, but the post-war impacts on strategy by the new government were interesting as well. In 1919, immediately after the Treaty of Versailles, the new German government was faced with defining the role of the navy within the confines of the Treaty of Versailles. Although the treaty permitted a very restricted navy, there were some in the Government who were willing to restrict it further. A proposal was made to limit the Germany Navy to nothing more than a coastal police force. Dr. Werner Rahn, a German naval officer, and historian, wrote in *The Navy and National Defense 1919-1928:*

> The reconstruction of a fleet must be renounced, because otherwise, "the mistrust of the world against Germany" will be kept, and above all, the honest international understanding of both parties in the Entente nations would be pushed off of us. The existing naval forces should only fulfill maritime law enforcement roles, such as patrolling the coast.[15]

This was the thinking of key elements in the early post-war government. Obviously, the threat to the existence of the German navy was not only present outside the borders.

The reduction in size of the German Navy was an obvious measure to prevent it from threatening the other nations in Europe. However, if the rest of Europe felt so threatened by the German Navy, then why not abolish it completely? Apparently, the authors of the Treaty of Versailles had something else in mind. In *The Navy and the Republic,* an article in *Characteristics of German Military History,* Dr. Rahn wrote that:

> The victors still had an interest to keep the German fleet as strong as possible, so that it could act as a stabilizing force in the confused situation in the Baltic.[16]

Even as the German government attempted to further reduce the role of the German Navy, the very nations who had forced the reductions on Germany still had reason for German seapower to remain in existence. The threat of Bolshevism from the Soviet Union was a threat that the victors of World War I became concerned with at the end of the war. The Baltic provided an avenue for a growing Soviet Navy to spread its influence further to the west. The German Navy, even in its reduced state would, if nothing else, alert Great Britain and France of the growing presence of a Soviet fleet in the Baltic. At best, it could act as a blocking force until more powerful naval forces from other countries could be dispatched. This is a concrete example of the confusion that existed regarding the strategic purpose for the German navy following the end of the First World War.

By the end of the twenties, the German Navy found itself with a plan to develop a larger, more capable navy. However, the constraints imposed by the Treaty of Versailles prohibited the open expansion of the German Navy. Instead of an open naval expansion program, the Germans embarked on a secret course of developing what they viewed as prospective naval technology in other countries. This development continued to reflect a Mahanian view on naval strategy, as the German plan was to build a multi-faceted fleet, complete with battleships, cruisers, submarines, and even aircraft carriers. This reflects Mahan's dictum of building the largest fleet possible, and building with the idea of engaging in a decisive large-scale battle at sea, with the goal being to vanquish the enemy's fleet.

Thus far, this thesis has examined the early history of the German Navy and its developing strategy. The early influence of Bismarck and Tirpitz on the strategy of the German navy, and its role in Europe were also reviewed. The impact of the First World War on the German Navy was discussed, and the efforts to overcome the restrictions of the Treaty of Versailles were reviewed. The following chapter will look at the efforts to rebuild the German Navy after 1930. Particular attention will be given to the influence that the two most prominent maritime theorists of that time had on the German Navy. Also, the impact of the 1935 Anglo-German Naval Agreement on German naval strategy will be reviewed.

---

[1]Gordon A. Craig, *Germany 1866-1945*, (New York: Oxford University Press, 1978), 228. This quote from Waldersee, who was the successor to von Moltke, gives a clear indication of the military's impression of the abilities of their new emperor.

[2]Ibid., 306

[3]Ibid., 304

[4]Ibid., 306

[5] Ibid., 308

[6] Ibid., 308

[7] Ibid., 313. There were many senior officials in England who were actually seeking an Anglo-German alliance. However, between Tirpitz's drive to build a large navy, and the Kaiser's erratic behavior, their desired alliance became less and less likely.

[8] Ibid., 309

[9] Ibid., 326

[10] John Keegan, *The First World War*, (New York: Alfred A. Knopf, 1999), pp 257-274

[11] Craig, 369

[12] Keegan, 351

[13] Ibid., 353-354

[14] Raeder, 140. Then Commander Canaris, who would later become the head of the German counter-intelligence branch used his personal contacts with the Spanish King to get a German submarine built in Cadiz. As a result of the Spanish Civil War, this submarine was eventually sold to Turkey. Later Canaris would be implicated as a member of the German resistance.

[15] Werner Rahn, *The Navy and defense of the Nation, 1919-1928*, (Munich: Bernard & Graefe Publishers for Military Studies, 1975). pp 35-36. Translation by author.

[16] Karl-Volker Neugebauer, ed., *Historical Overview,* vol 1 of *Characteristics of German Military History*, Werner Rahn (Freiburg in Breisgau: Rombach Verlag, 1993), pg 294. Translation by author.

CHAPTER 4

A GERMAN MAHANIAN NAVY

The German Navy continued through the twenties to build those ships and

weapons system permitted, and to secretly develop those it could not. The navy always

desired to build a bigger navy, but was constrained externally by the Treaty of Versailles,

and internally by governments that were not prepared to challenge the treaty. The secret

development programs were the only avenues available to the German Navy to grow and

develop beyond the confines of the treaty. Their selection of technologies was reflective

of their view of the strategic employment of the Navy. The Navy's vision was of a large

fleet, with a multitude of capabilities that would sail from its home port to engage an

enemy fleet on the high seas. This reflects a continued Mahanian perspective on the

employment of a navy. This would be the view of the navy for some time to come.

From 1930 until 1933, Germany continued to be limited in the size of its armed

forces by the Treaty of Versailles. Therefore, they were still prohibited from building

certain kinds of weapons systems (submarines, aircraft, and battleships, to name a few).

However, the covert program of research started in the 1920s continued into the 1930s.

Not only was the building of the armed forces restricted, but the strategic purpose of the

armed forces was limited as well. The strategic purpose of the German Navy discussed in

the last chapter remained the official strategy in the new decade.

It was not until 1933 that the Navy veered from its previous course. The

appointment of Adolph Hitler as German chancellor had two immediate impacts on the

German Navy. First, he stated that one of his most important goals was the rearmament of Germany.[1] Next, he reaffirmed Raeder's desire to keep Great Britain from becoming an enemy of Germany. These two goals would help steer the course of the German navy for several years.

Rearmament

Hitler's commitment to increasing the size of the German Armed Forces provided the opportunity to increase the level of technological innovation that the Navy pursued over the previous decade. Hitler's open support for military enlargement was a contrast to previous political administrations, including the Weimar Republic. Not only did it increase the political support for the military, but it was also a significant boon to the morale of the members of the Armed Forces. They now had a political leader who gave them his wholehearted support. Further, along with Hitler's political support came the financial support necessary to expand the research projects the navy was conducting.

The platforms that the German Navy developed immediately after 1933 illuminate the strategic approach they were taking. Because the Treaty of Versailles limited not only the type of ships that the German Navy could build, but also their size, the main capital ships Germany built in the twenties and early thirties were not battleships as they were defined. Rather, they were called "pocket battleships." Armed with 28-centimeter guns, displacing no more than 10,000 tons and having a top speed of 26 knots, they were the limit of what Germany could build under the constraints of Versailles. By way of comparison, the French Navy was building the *Dunkerque* class of battle cruiser which boasted 33-centimeter guns, displacements of 26,500 tons, and top speeds of 30 knots.

The fact that they were severely constrained in what they could build had an impact on their strategic thinking. The German Navy viewed France as their most likely opponent in a future conflict. Therefore, even under the constraints of Versailles, they were aware that conditions would most likely change at some point in the future. The German Navy was attempting to build a fleet that could challenge the French on the open seas, and engage them in a decisive battle. This is an example of an entirely Mahanian view of naval warfare.

Once Hitler was appointed, the German Navy commenced the initial stages of planning for a class of battleship that would meet, or exceed, the capabilities of the other nations in Europe. A ship displacing in excess of 30,000 tons, equipped with 38-centimeter guns. The propulsion for these ships turned out to be one of the most contested issues. German industry had developed a diesel engine suited for shipboard use that provided a very long cruising range, and adequate speed. However, many power stations on shore were using new oil-fired steam turbines. Raeder thought that a maritime version would allow for a higher speed with lower weight. But before this new class of ship could actually be built, the restrictions of the Versailles treaty would have to be removed.

Battleships were not the only naval technology under development. Germany spent a great deal of effort improving on the design of submarines. Submarines had a significant impact in the First World War. After an attempt at a form of legal submarine warfare directed against the allies early in the war, followed by a period of more restricted submarine warfare, Germany eventually declared unconditional submarine warfare in 1917. Submarines began attacking allied merchant vessels and met with significant success until the allies began using the convoy system. Attacking an enemy's lines of communication in an effort to restrict their ability to produce war material or feed themselves is an example of Corbett's theory of maritime warfare rather than Mahan's.

33

The attempted use of submarines in a decisive battle against an enemy fleet was planned for Jutland. However, the submarines failed to find the British fleet. The attempt to employ submarines in accordance with Mahan's theory of maritime warfare had failed. The experience of the German Navy regarding submarines was that they met with much more success in attacks against enemy merchant vessels than as part of a battle fleet. The German Navy applied these lessons to their efforts to develop the submarine.

Aviation was another area that the German navy attempted to exploit. As with submarines, the German navy was forbidden to posses or build aircraft. And just like submarines, they went to other countries to begin secret development of a forbidden technology. As was the case with battleships, Hitler's rise to power allowed the navy to pursue a more robust aviation program. Raeder eventually envisioned a German Navy that included aircraft carriers, and a substantial naval aviation force. However, the main opponent of the development of naval aviation was neither the Allies, nor traditional officers in the Navy; rather, the greatest obstacle to the development of naval aviation was Marshall Hermann Goering, head of the Luftwaffe. He stated that anything that flew in the German Armed Forces would belong to the Luftwaffe. Despite the best attempts of Raeder, all aviation remained under the control of the Luftwaffe. Goering did establish a few aviation squadrons that were supposed to be dedicated to maritime purposes, however, not in the numbers that the Navy deemed necessary to be effective.[2]

The question then becomes to which maritime theory did naval aviation belong at this stage? Unlike battleships and submarines, there was no major battle in which aircraft participated. The technology had not sufficiently developed to allow aircraft to exert a major impact in maritime combat. However, their potential was widely recognized. In the

34

United States, Billy Mitchell sank several stationary battleships from the air, demonstrating potential ability of aircraft to impact a battle at sea. Combined with the intention of building aircraft carriers, it is apparent that the German Navy saw value in the capability to engage an enemy fleet with naval air forces. As evidenced by their intended use of battleships and submarines, it follows that their intention was to use aircraft carriers as part of a fleet designed to engage their adversaries at sea. This is another example of the application of Mahan's theories.

The German Navy was proceeding along the lines of Mahan's ideas of developing a fleet. The weapons systems that they were pursuing were designed with the goal of building the most capable fleet possible, and being able to achieve a decisive victory over an enemy's fleet at sea in a massive battle and render that fleet useless. Hitler's support was critical to the Navy's pursuit of expanding its planning for a larger fleet at such a time when it might be released from the confines of the Treaty of Versailles.

Great Britain

As the German Navy had been developing and building a fleet in accordance with Mahan's theories, it was critical to keep Great Britain from becoming a potentially hostile power. Raeder knew that there was no way that the German Navy could oppose the Royal Navy in its current state, or for the foreseeable future. Therefore, if Germany was going to build the best fleet possible with the intent of decisively defeating another fleet at sea, Great Britain could not be counted as an adversary. Any attempt to fight the British at sea would lead only to disaster.

Along with fostering the rearmament of the German Armed forces, Hitler provided another invaluable service to the German Navy. In their first meeting in 1933,

Raeder emphasized to Hitler the need to keep Great Britain from becoming an enemy. Hitler responded by stating that it was his intent to do everything possible to maintain good relations with Great Britain. However, in March 1935, Hitler repudiated the military clauses of the treaty of Versailles. Immediately thereafter, he reinstituted mandatory military conscription[3], and subsequently the restrictions placed on the German Armed Forces regarding developing arms in secret were lifted.

Hitler anticipated the alarm that this would cause in Great Britain, and had already begun discussing measures to allay British fears. As early as 1934, Hitler had mentioned to visiting British diplomats that Germany would be willing to enter into a naval agreement with the United Kingdom. A tonnage ratio of 100:35 was discussed and both parties agreed to consider the proposal further. After discussions with naval leadership, Hitler decided to act on his earlier discussions with the British and to pursue a naval treaty with Great Britain

The Anglo-German Naval Treaty of 1935 was seen as a success for both countries. The British saw it as a concession by the Germans to British naval supremacy. Wilhelm II's policy of naval expansion was seen by many in Great Britain as one of the main causes of the First World War. So, by voluntarily limiting their fleet to roughly a third of the size of the Royal Navy, the British viewed the treaty very favorably. The Germans would not pursue a reckless program of naval expansion as had been the case at the turn of the century.

From the German point of view, the treaty was also a success for more than one reason. First, it provided a form of international recognition to Hitler's repudiation of the military clauses of the Treaty of Versailles. Hitler had unilaterally renounced those clauses in March 1935, without the consent of any of the signatories of the treaty which created them. By having the British agree to the treaty, Hitler achieved international recognition that the treaty was, at least in part, invalidated. Even with only thirty-five percent of the tonnage of the Royal Navy, the German Navy would still gain a significant amount of available tonnage. The ships that existed only on the drafting table could now be built. Also, the Germans gained the right to build up to forty-five percent of the Royal Navy's tonnage of submarines. Not only that, but they also had a caveat in the treaty permitting them to build up to one hundred percent of the Royal Navy's tonnage of submarines if they felt necessary. The only caveat in the treaty was that the Germans should notify the British if they were going to build excess submarines. Finally, this treaty ensured good relations between Great Britain and Germany. This was the critical point for German Naval strategy; with Great Britain now as a non-hostile power, Germany could continue down the path of developing a Mahanian Navy. The vision of building a fleet with aircraft carriers, aircraft, battleships, and submarines could now be openly pursued.

At the end of 1935 the German Navy found itself freed of the constraints of the Treaty of Versailles to the extent that it could openly develop military technology prohibited after the First World War. The treaty with Great Britain in 1935 secured not only the right to expand the size of the navy, but also ensured that the navy could focus its efforts on building a navy capable of engaging a hostile fleet with a significant chance of victory.

Another strategic impact of the Anglo-German Naval Agreement was its effect on the size of the German Navy in relation to the size of the Italian and French Fleets. The

French and Italian Navies were participants in the earlier Washington Naval Treaty of 1922. This treaty limited the size of their navies, as well as the size of the Royal Navy, Japanese Navy, and U.S. Navy. When the British agreed to the terms of the Anglo-German Naval Agreement, they effectively granted parity to the German Navy with the Italian and French Navies. As the Germans had always seen France as their next potential enemy, this was a significant advantage to Germany.[4]

In the middle of 1935, Germany's secret rearmament program came to an end. In 1936, the German Navy erased any possible doubts about its intentions. The keels were laid for the battleships *Bismarck* and *Tirpitz*, in Hamburg and Wilhelmshaven. Their official standard displacement was 35,000 tons, however, 42,000 was a more realistic figure. When fully loaded and fueled, they would displace 52,600 tons. Armed with eight 38-centimeter guns, and twelve 15-centimeter guns, powered by high pressure steam turbines capable of driving the ship to 31 knots, and with a range of 8,000 nautical miles, these were battleships by any definition, and arguably, would be among the most advanced warships in the world once complete.[5] However, battleships were not the only new ships of the German Navy. The plan that had existed on paper to build a balanced fleet could now be openly put into effect. Continuing in the Mahanian tradition, the German Navy now began to build a large multipurpose fleet.

This chapter has discussed the influences on the German Navy from 1930 to 1936. The covert program to develop technology in other nations, which started in the 1920s continued into the 1930s. By examining the kinds of ships the German Navy wanted to build, their purposed can be deduced. Furthermore, by knowing why the German Navy was planning on building certain kinds of ships, the level of influence of the two main maritime theorists is readily apparent. The impact of the rise of Hitler, his policy of military expansion, and his influence on naval strategy were reviewed. The effect of the Anglo-German Naval Treaty of 1935 on the German Navy was the last factor in this chapter. The next, and final, chapter will discuss the conclusions that can be drawn from the third and fourth chapters, and will make recommendations for further research.

---

[1]Thomas, 79. The army proved to be the initial benefactor of Hitler's increased military budget. Raeder immediately sought to rectify the imbalance.

[2]Vice Admiral Friedrich Ruge, *Der Seekrieg* (Annapolis: United States Naval Institute, 1957), 47.

[3]Craig, 608.

[4]Emily O. Goldman, *Sunken Treaties, Naval Arms Control Between the Wars* (University Park: The Pennsylvania State University Press, 1994), 227-228.

[5]Ruge, 30.

CHAPTER 5

CONCLUSIONS AND RECOMMENDATIONS

From the time of Kaiser Wilhelm II to 1936, Germany built, lost, and then rebuilt a navy. The technology involved, the cost of the ships, and the strategic implications of having a navy demanded considerable thought and planning. Theorists had written about war on land for centuries. Frederick the Great, Jomini, and Clausewitz are a few of the authors whose works had significant impacts on the development of armies throughout history. The end of the nineteenth century saw the first significant maritime theorist, Alfred Thayer Mahan, publish *The Influence of Seapower on History*. Sir Julian Corbett followed with *Some Principles of Maritime Strategy*. So, what influence did these men have on the development of strategy by the German Navy?

Certainly, Mahan was the more influential at first, partially because his book was published first. Not only was timing in Mahan's favor, but Wilhelm II was, to put it mildly, a naval enthusiast. His familial ties to England, his admiration of the Royal Navy, and his view of himself as a military expert all contributed to his support of the development of the German Navy. He used *The Influence of Seapower Upon History* as his guide, and thus set out to build the largest fleet he could. Wilhelm II's fleet represented the best technology that Germany had, and was a multi-faceted fleet, complete with battleships, armored cruisers, and submarines. The Kaiser wanted his fleet to be at least the equal of Great Britain's.

This fleet did not meet with the success he had hoped for during its engagements in World War I. In fact the largest naval engagement of World War I, the Battle of

Jutland, proved to be much less decisive than either side had hoped. From a strictly numerical view, the German Navy inflicted a greater number of casualties than they suffered. However, the German surface fleet as a whole was out of action for the remainder of the war. Not only did the Kaiser's Navy not meet his expectations, but Mahan's great battle at sea did not occur the way he envisioned it. The Imperial Navy did not remain in port for the remainder of the war because it had been soundly defeated at sea; rather, it remained in port because of the decisions of the Kaiser. Further, the branch of the Navy that had the greatest impact on the Allies was the submarine force. When submarines were used as part of a battle fleet, as they were at Jutland, they had limited effect. However, when used as commerce raiders, they created significant pressure on Great Britain. At the end of World War I, the Kaiser's Navy failed where he foresaw success, and succeeded where it was not expected to.

Up to World War I, Mahan had almost exclusive dominance in the development of German naval strategy. The Kaiser's pursuit of a large multi-purpose navy prior to World War I clearly demonstrated his agreement with Mahan. However, after World War I, the German Navy began to show an appreciation for at least some new ways of looking at naval strategy. The effort put into the submarine program is a prime example. World War I showed beyond doubt that the submarine was most effective against merchant vessels. The fact that Germany went to such great lengths to develop a weapons system that was directed at merchant vessels is clearly an indication that they were beginning to accept alternatives to Mahan's views.

As stated earlier, the German Fleet did not meet with the level success hoped for at the Battle of Jutland. In spite of this, the continued pursuit of large warships, as limited as they were by the Treaty of Versailles, indicated that the German Navy still believed that fleets would meet on the seas, and engage in combat. They continued to dedicate the resources they had available to a large extent towards the building and development of battleships and battle cruisers, which they expected to use in a fleet on fleet role. This was still very much a Mahanian outlook on maritime warfare.

This process continued through the early 1930s. The German Navy continued to pursue a predominantly Mahanian approach towards building a fleet, but not entirely so. There were advocates of conducting maritime warfare according to Corbett's theories. Admiral Doenitz, for example, believed that a key element in a maritime conflict with England would be an attack on her merchant shipping. The continued effort to develop submarines, and their tactics, which were directed at conducting attacks on convoys were indications of this. However, the dominant portion of their resources and efforts went toward the building of a large multi-purpose fleet. The launching of the *Graf Spee* class, and *Scharnhorst* class, and laying of *Tirpitz* and *Bismarck* were unmistakable signs that the German Navy continued to place great value in the Mahanian theory of building the biggest fleet possible for the purpose of decisively engaging, then defeating, an enemy fleet at sea.

The type of ships built was not the only element of naval strategy that was important to the German Navy. Admiral Erich Raeder, head of the German Navy from 1928 to 1943, had made a priority in all of his dealings with the various governments he served with to ensure that Great Britain not become an enemy. He knew that the German Navy wouldn't be capable of defeating the Royal Navy at sea. In all of the exercises and war games the German Navy conducted, he went to great lengths to not name Great

Britain as the opposing force. After Hitler came to power, Germany went one step further. In 1935, Germany and Great Britain signed a naval agreement that permitted Germany to build to thirty-five percent of the tonnage of the Royal Navy, and up to forty-five percent of the tonnage of the Royal Navy in submarines. The agreement had several effects. First, it was a very reassuring sign to Great Britain that Germany was not going to repeat the naval arms race prior to World War I. Next, it permitted Germany to significantly expand her naval building program. Another effect of the agreement was that it provided an international form of recognition that Germany was freed from the military restrictions of the Treaty of Versailles.

After signing the agreement, Germany's military research and development programs, which had been previously carried out covertly in other countries, were moved out in the open. In 1936, the keels were laid for the largest battleships the German Navy had ever built, *Tirpitz* and *Bismarck*. This was the capstone event for the German Navy regarding their building program. Finally, they were openly constructing new ships that were on par, if not superior, to those of every other navy in the world. These ships represented a powerful statement, which was that Germany intended to compete on par with the rest of the world. They were built to fulfill the Mahanian role of engaging an enemy fleet at sea and rendering a single decisive battle, eliminating the enemy fleet as threat for the rest of the war. However, these ships could also be used as merchant raiders, fulfilling some of Corbett's views on naval warfare.

Conclusions

After examining the historical development of the German Navy, in particular its strategy and strategic views, certain conclusions are clear. The influence of Mahan on the

German Navy is obvious. The Kaiser read Mahan's work frequently himself, as did most of his senior staff. The naval building program that Admiral Tirpitz proposed to the government in 1898, and again in 1901 reflected a very Mahanian view of building a navy. The German Fleet was built to be able to challenge Great Britain's Royal Navy. The purpose of the fleet was to be able to defeat the Royal Navy at sea, clearly adhering to Mahan's precepts. The Kaiser took his navy to war with England, and in the only large scale naval engagement of the war, achieved only a minor tactical success. In fact, the German High Seas fleet was kept in port for the remainder of the war.

Did this outcome nullify Mahan's theories? If the German Navy achieved tactical success, then why did it not leave port in force for the remainder of the war? The reason the fleet did not leave port for the remainder of the war was a result of the decisions of the Kaiser. Having seen six ships sunk in the Battle of Jutland, the Kaiser decided that the fleet was at too much risk to send to sea again in force. The problem was not the inaccuracy of Mahan's theory of a decisive battle at sea, rather the refusal of a monarch to risk his fleet in pursuing it. Having achieved a tactical victory over the Royal Navy, the argument can be made that the German Navy could have sought out the Royal Navy again to finish what they had started at Jutland.

As stated earlier, the performance of the battleships was not the only event that reflected on the validity of maritime theory. Although ineffective at Jutland, the submarine campaign, especially when unrestricted submarine warfare was declared, became the most effective maritime element of the German effort during World War I. The ability of the submarines to interdict supplies coming to Great Britain undeniably was a reflection of Corbett's theories.

What effect did the First World War have on the German Navy's view of Mahan and Corbett? Based on the evidence in chapters three and four, the German Navy still held to Mahan's theories, as demonstrated by their efforts to build a large fleet, comprised of capital ships. However, the effort and resources dedicated to the development of a submarine force clearly show that the German Navy was aware of the lessons learned from the submarine campaign of World War I. If a submarine force the size of the World War I force had the effect that it did, then how much more effective would a larger force have been? Looking at the results achieved in World War I, the German Navy embraced Corbett's views with respect to commerce raiding and sea lines of communication interdiction.

Finally, what effect did maritime theorists have on the development of German naval strategy from 1930 to 1936? The German Navy applied the lessons learned from World War I, and used the theories of both Mahan and Corbett, where appropriate. The German Navy's overall goal was to produce a large fleet to the extent possible, first under the Treaty of Versailles, then under the auspices of the 1935 London Naval Agreement. The main fleet was to be a multi-purpose fleet capable of defeating an enemy at sea decisively. However, considerable effort was dedicated to a submarine force whose goal was the interdiction of merchant vessels. These somewhat divergent efforts indicate the ability of the leadership of the German Navy to not tie themselves to one theory; rather to find the value in each and apply them as they felt appropriate.

Relevance

The discussion of this subject is very interesting for historians. However, it is entirely valid to ask what relevance this subject has today. The historical case study used to examine the influence of naval theorists in developing a maritime strategy involved a navy that was in a significant state of transition during a period of political turmoil. All of these factors can be found today.

The United States spent enormous amounts of effort and resources to build a military that would be capable of engaging in combat against the former Soviet Union. However, the Soviet Union ceased to exist in the early nineties. The United States Armed Forces were very quickly deprived not only of their primary opponent, but also the model on which strategy, doctrine, and size were founded. It is certainly arguable that this effect was most profound on the Navy, because the number of countries that can afford to maintain a navy are drastically less than the number that can afford armies. Also, those countries that can afford to maintain navies are mostly our allies.

In the period since the fall of the Soviet Union, the United States Navy has been faced with the challenge of redefining itself. Gone are the days when fleet planners anticipated large scale battles at sea with carrier battlegroups defending themselves against Soviet bombers, submarines, and ship launched anti-ship cruise missiles. With the Soviet threat gone, what purpose would the United States Navy need to fulfill? Have the leaders of the United States Navy planned a strategy based on the theories of Corbett or Mahan?

The United States Navy continues to build aircraft carriers and the modern version of the capital ship, the Ticonderoga class guided missile cruiser. The modern escort is the Arliegh Burke class guided missile destroyer. The capabilities between the two ships are remarkable similar. The striking power of the carrier battle group centers on the embarked airwing, and the cruise missile capability of the accompanying cruisers and destroyers. When fast attack submarines are added to the mix, the carrier battle group represents unsurpassed maritime military capability. The carrier battle group is certainly capable of engaging in a major battle at sea against an opposing force. Although this capability exists, there is currently no equivalent opposing naval force. So, although the navy has the capability to engage in a Mahanian decisive battle at sea, the most important piece, the enemy, is missing. However, the large naval force in the modern era has a new capability; exerting power projection ashore.

Does this invalidate Mahan's theories for the United States Navy in today's operating environment? Mahan's six principle conditions still apply, but if there is no enemy to engage in a large battle at sea, do his theories have any use? Although there is no large naval force capable of engaging the United States Navy in an all out decisive battle at sea, it is difficult to foresee the future. The capabilities of the navy, centered on the carrier battle group, will be the mainstay of the navy for the foreseeable future. A possible naval opponent could be developing today. Many regard China and India as possible nations that will eventually have navies capable of challenging ours. In this case, Mahan's battle at sea would be a distinct possibility requiring the naval capability that exists today. Rather than disregarding Mahan's theories, the prudent naval planner will continue to study them to be able to meet future requirements and threats.

With the collapse of the Soviet Union, and the development of the world's political structure since, many senior naval officers have seen the need for the navy to operate closer to the shore. Also, with the United States having an unprecedented level of command of the seas, the need for expending effort in this area has decreased. Most discussion of the use of the United States Navy today centers around the navy's ability to influence the land war. This is more in line with Corbett's theories than with Mahan's. However, the navy has yet to build a platform dedicated to this kind of warfare. The Tomahawk land attack missile does give the navy the ability to strike targets far inland, as does naval aviation, but these are systems that were adapted to new tasks. A strong argument can be made that the United States Navy is developing a strategy based more on Corbett's theories than on Mahan's. The increasing focus on influencing land war is evidence of this. The Expeditionary Strike Group and the Littoral Combat Ship are current concepts that show the influence of Corbett's ideas on naval thinking and strategy.[1]

In order to formulate a comprehensive strategy for the United States Navy, Admiral Vernon Clark, the Chief of Naval Operations, published Sea Power 21. This document provides his vision for how the United States Navy will develop in the coming decades. As stated earlier, the United States is retaining capabilities in line with Mahan's theories, but developing more capabilities and doctrine that reflect significant influence from Corbett. Not only does Sea Power 21 show the influence of maritime theorists on the modern United States Navy, but also points to new developments in naval strategy. Admiral Clark proposes a concept called "Sea Basing." This concept postulates the ability to creating mobile logistic bases that can be positioned wherever needed. This would have a significant impact on some of Mahan's six principle conditions, and impact on some of Corbett's theories as well.

Finally, do the new developments in technology demand a new theory of maritime warfare? Some of the concepts in Sea Power 21 certainly lead to the conclusion that maritime theory should change to meet the changes in naval technology and the modern geo-political environment, which would be hardly recognizable to either Mahan or Corbett.

Further Study

This thesis looked specifically at the period from 1930 to 1936 in order to capture the German Navy under the last of the Weimar Republic, and the rise of the NSDAP. Also, 1936 was chosen for the end because that would permit an examination of the Anglo-German Naval agreement, and the after effects it had on German shipbuilding. In 1936, Hitler was continuing to reassure Raeder that Great Britain would not become an enemy of Germany, and the battleships *Tirpitz* and *Bismarck* were laid. This thesis did not address the period of time beyond 1936. That timeframe would be an excellent area for further study because it includes the "Z-Plan," which demonstrates a significant shift in German Naval strategy.

Another area of further study would be the examination of the impact of Mahan and Corbett on the Royal Navy and United States Navy. As the main maritime opponents of Germany in World War I, it would be very enlightening to see to what extent their navies were influenced, and how those influences manifested themselves. Does their status as the victors imply that they had a better understanding of Mahan's and Corbett's theories? Or, was it a question of resources?

Finally, a study of the influence of Mahan and Corbett on the modern navies of the United States, Great Britain, and Germany would prove most valuable. To what extent are the current strategies of each navy influenced by Mahan and Corbett? Has the evolution of more modern weapon systems and command and control systems made their theories obsolete? If so, who has replaced Mahan and Corbett as the modern maritime

theorist? Or, is there a need for a new way of looking at maritime theory.

---

[1]Admiral Vernon Clark, "Sea Power 21," *Proceedings*, October 2002. 32-41.

APPENDIX A

TRANSLATION OF "DIE REICHSMARINE UND DIE REPUBLIK"

Dr. Werner Rahn
Aus: Grundzuege der deutschen Militaergescichte, Band 1: Historischer Ueberblick,
HRSG. Volker Neugebauer, Freiburg, S.294-299

The Transition Phase

In view of the severe defeat, the internal unrest, and the armed disagreement with Poland, the German naval armed forces appeared at first extremely superfluous. Still, the victorious powers had an interest to keep the German fleet as strong as possible so that it could be used as a maritime stabilization force in view of the confused situation in the Baltic. In accordance with the peace treaty, the German naval forces were not permitted beyond the following size: six older capital ships, six light cruisers, twelve destroyers, and 12 torpedo boats. Submarines and military aircraft were generally forbidden. Therefore the navy was lacking modern weapons systems without which a future war at sea seemed unthinkable. The permitted naval forces were only allowed to be replaced with predefined displacement according to a fixed age list. The limit on personnel was fixed at 15000 long-term volunteers.

During the difficult struggle regarding the question of accepting or denying the peace treaty, the navy became a national symbol against the Allies with the unauthorized scuttling of the fleet at Scappa Flow on June 21, 1919. In this act, the naval leadership saw, above all else, a moral act which should form a basis for the rebuilding of the navy.

After the collapse of 1918 and the delivery of the fleet, disintegration and loss of discipline appeared which was contradicted by the training of volunteer units in 1919.

51

Next to a few mine hunting flotillas, three Naval brigades were kept as additional government troops because of their isolated nature and stress on strict discipline. Admittedly, they proceeded on their missions in the internal areas with brutal harshness, not finally with the motivation to lift the, since November 1918, damaged image of the Navy. Two naval brigades were formed with radical nationalistic thoughts; the troops were not prepared to accept defeat, and had no understanding for the difficult situation of the government, whose posture with regard to the Allies as "Politics of Satisfaction" was smeared (ridiculed?) The latent danger existed that both of these brigades would get out of political control and become a danger for the young republic. That happened in early 1920.

Under the pressure of Allied demands, the reduction of the Armed Forces defined in the peace treaty became inevitable in March 1920. The government ordered the dissolution of the naval brigades. Leading military members and radical right wing leaders (powers), who did not want to put up with that, used military measures to apply pressure to the government (Kapp-Luettwitz revolt). The navy played a special role in these improvised coup attempts: The second naval brigade (Ehrhardt) was the most important instrument of power of the rebels in Berlin and, in contrast to the contradictory behavior of the army leadership, the navy, with Vice Admiral v. Trotha the head of the admiralty, openly acknowledged that the navy was at the service of the new government. This disloyal conduct towards the legal government gave rise to the energetic resistance of numerous Deck Officers, Petty Officers, and seaman and led to the violent removal of Officers in most naval units especially in Kiel where there were many bloody street fights.

Trotha and his advisors had a concept of the political neutrality of the navy that would be incomprehensible for us today. Whether a change of government occurred constitutionally or violently was irrelevant. Many officers advocated the view that overthrow of 1918 was illegal, but still accepted the fait accompli. If another successful revolt occurred and there was yet another fait accompli, it would have fit the military leadership. In this line of thinking, the form and constitutionality of a government became secondary in comparison to the purely military goal of the preservation of functioning armed forces. Trotha wanted to maintain the inner coherence of the navy through his apparent neutrality, but achieved the opposite because he inaccurately assessed the political attitude of most of the Deck Officers and Petty officers as well as the civilian workers in the large naval garrisons.

Immediately after the collapse of the revolt, Trotha was removed from his office. His interim successor, Rear Admiral Michaelis, inherited a scrap heap. He had to have realized that the political position of the navy after the disaster of the revolt was "seemingly bad and weak," or worse to the extent that its existence was threatened. In August 1920, he succeeded with great skill to secure a decision from the government cabinet that secured the continued existence of the navy and their independence within the armed forces. During his military arguments, the necessity of a coastal defense force and the securing of the sea passages to eastern Prussia definitively influenced the decision. After the clarification of the question of the continued existence of the navy, the navy needed some time to consolidate. The first chief of the Naval Staff, Admiral Behncke certainly had considerable difficulties with the integration of the members of the former naval brigades from 1920-1923, who intentionally made their radical political views known and with them provoked a lot of political incidents. This sort of occurrence resulted in a justified mistrust with the democratic parties. The navy was justifiably called the "Nursery of the Reactionary."

APPENDIX B

TRANSLATION OF THE NAVY AND NATIONAL DEFENSE, 1919-1928,
CHAPTER 2, SECTION I

Dr. Werner Rahn

Early military-political ideas in the navy prior to the peace treaty

Early in 1919, the first realizations inside the navy arose of the future roles the new and small navy could be assigned within the German Defense and Foreign policies and with which concepts these roles might be carried out.

The Hamburg Congress of the Sailors advisory council demanded a radical change of concept for the navy. In one of the national directed meetings, a naval program was formulated that was strongly formed in its political, economic, and military demands by the socialist ideas of the 53 committee. The "adaptation of the changed world situation" made the "dismantling of a German power and world policy" necessary. The rebuilding of a fleet had to be renounced, lest otherwise "the mistrust of the world of Germany" would remain vigilant and above all else "honest international understanding of the Entennte nations would be pushed away from us." The existing naval armed forces should only fill the maritime law enforcement role of "patrolling the coast," unless the peace conference decided about the "Creation of a sea power as part of the world executive." An "effective Socialist" had to appointed be as state secretary of the RMA (Reichs Marine Amt) with the obligation to dismiss all "somehow superfluous and … reactionary Officers and Officials." The naval facilities, which had previously served exclusively military goals (for example shipyards and workshops), were supposed to be better used for the general economy and be reorganized according to better business

practices.

BIBLIOGRAPHY

Birdsall, Paul. *Versailles Twenty Years After*. Hamden: Archons Books, 1962.

Blair, Clay. *Hitler's U-Boat War: The Hunters, 1939-1942*. New York: Random House, 1996.

Clark, Vernon, Admiral. "Sea Power 21." *Proceedings*, October 2002, 32-41.

Corbett, Julian Stafford. *Some Principles of Maritime Strategy*. Annapolis: Naval Institute Press, 1988.

Craig, Gordon A. *Germany, 1866-1945*. New York: Oxford University Press, 1978.

Goldman, Emily O. *Sunken Treaties: Naval Arms Control Between the Wars*. University Park: The Pennsylvania State University Press, 1994.

Keegan, John. *The First World War*. New York: Alfred A. Knopf, 1998.

_____. *The Second World War*. New York: Penguin Books USA, 1989.

Mahan, Alfred Thayer. *The Influence of Sea Power upon History: 1660-1783*. New York: Hill and Wang, 1957.

Mallmann Showell, Jak P. *German Navy Handbook, 1939-1945*. Gloucestershire: Sutton Publishing Limited, 1999.

Mortenssen, Anthony. *Hitler and His Admirals*. New York: E. P. Dutton and Co., 1949.

Murray, Williamson, and Allan R. Millett. eds. *Military Innovation in the Interwar Period*. New York: Cambridge University Press, 1996.

Neugebauer, Karl-Volger. *Grundzuegu der deutschen Militaergeschichte, Bd 1*, Freiburg im Breisgau: Rombach Verlag, 1993.

Paret, Peter. Makers of Modern Strategy from Machiavelli to the Nuclear Age. Princeton: Princeton University Press, 1986.

Parker, Geoffrey, ed. *Cambridge Illustrated History: Warfare*. Cambridge: Cambridge University Press, 1995.

Rahn, Werner. *Kriegfuehrung, Politik, Krisen - Die Marine des Deutschen Reiches 1914-1933*. In: Die deutsche Flotte im Spannungsfeld der Politik, 1848-1985. Herford: Deutsches Marine Institut und Militaergeschichtliches Forschungsamt, 1985.

Reader, Erich. *Grand Admiral*, Annapolis: Naval Institute Press, 1969.

Ruge, Friedrich. *Der Seekrieg*. Annapolis: United States Naval Institute, 1957.

Salewski, Michael. *Das maritime Dritte Reich - Ideologie und Wirklichkeit, 1933-1945*. Herford: Deutsches Marine Institut und Militaergeschichtliches Forschungsamt, 1985.

Tarrant, V. E. *Jutland: The German Perspective*. Annapolis: Naval Institute Press, 1997.

Thomas, Charles S. *The German Navy in the Nazi Era*. Annapolis: Naval Institute Press, 1990.

INITIAL DISTRIBUTION LIST

Combined Arms Research Library
U.S. Army Command and General Staff College
250 Gibbon Ave.
Fort Leavenworth, KS 66027-2314

Defense Technical Information Center/OCA
825 John J. Kingman Rd., Suite 944
Fort Belvoir, VA 22060-6218

CDR John T. Kuehn
USNE
USACGSC
1 Reynolds Ave.
Fort Leavenworth, KS 66027-1352

LTC Edward L. Bowie
CSI
USACGSC
1 Reynolds Ave.
Fort Leavenworth, KS 66027-1352

COL Kendra K. Kattelmann
Consulting Faculty, DGDP
USACGSC
1 Reynolds Ave.
Fort Leavenworth, KS 66027-1352

CERTIFICATION FOR MMAS DISTRIBUTION STATEMENT

1. Certification Date: 18 June 2004

2. Thesis Author: LCDR Donald A. Cribbs

3. Thesis Title: The Influence of Maritime Theorists on the Development of German Naval Strategy from 1930 to 1936

4. Thesis Committee Members: _____

   Signatures: _____

   _____

5. Distribution Statement: See distribution statements A-X on reverse, then circle appropriate distribution statement letter code below:

(A) B C D E F X   SEE EXPLANATION OF CODES ON REVERSE

If your thesis does not fit into any of the above categories or is classified, you must coordinate with the classified section at CARL.

6. Justification: Justification is required for any distribution other than described in Distribution Statement A. All or part of a thesis may justify distribution limitation. See limitation justification statements 1-10 on reverse, then list, below, the statement(s) that applies (apply) to your thesis and corresponding chapters/sections and pages. Follow sample format shown below:

EXAMPLE

Limitation Justification Statement	/	Chapter/Section	/	Page(s)
Direct Military Support (10)	/	Chapter 3	/	12
Critical Technology (3)	/	Section 4	/	31
Administrative Operational Use (7)	/	Chapter 2	/	13-32

Fill in limitation justification for your thesis below:

Limitation Justification Statement	/	Chapter/Section	/	Page(s)
_____	/	_____	/	_____
_____	/	_____	/	_____
_____	/	_____	/	_____
_____	/	_____	/	_____
_____	/	_____	/	_____

7. MMAS Thesis Author's Signature: _____

60

STATEMENT A: Approved for public release; distribution is unlimited. (Documents with this statement may be made available or sold to the general public and foreign nationals).

STATEMENT B: Distribution authorized to U.S. Government agencies only (insert reason and date ON REVERSE OF THIS FORM). Currently used reasons for imposing this statement include the following:

    1. Foreign Government Information. Protection of foreign information.

    2. Proprietary Information. Protection of proprietary information not owned by the U.S. Government.

    3. Critical Technology. Protection and control of critical technology including technical data with potential military application.

    4. Test and Evaluation. Protection of test and evaluation of commercial production or military hardware.

    5. Contractor Performance Evaluation. Protection of information involving contractor performance evaluation.

    6. Premature Dissemination. Protection of information involving systems or hardware from premature dissemination.

    7. Administrative/Operational Use. Protection of information restricted to official use or for administrative or operational purposes.

    8. Software Documentation. Protection of software documentation - release only in accordance with the provisions of DoD Instruction 7930.2.

    9. Specific Authority. Protection of information required by a specific authority.

    10. Direct Military Support. To protect export-controlled technical data of such military significance that release for purposes other than direct support of DoD-approved activities may jeopardize a U.S. military advantage.

STATEMENT C: Distribution authorized to U.S. Government agencies and their contractors: (REASON AND DATE). Currently most used reasons are 1, 3, 7, 8, and 9 above.

STATEMENT D: Distribution authorized to DoD and U.S. DoD contractors only; (REASON AND DATE). Currently most reasons are 1, 3, 7, 8, and 9 above.

STATEMENT E: Distribution authorized to DoD only; (REASON AND DATE). Currently most used reasons are 1, 2, 3, 4, 5, 6, 7, 8, 9, and 10.

STATEMENT F: Further dissemination only as directed by (controlling DoD office and date), or higher DoD authority. Used when the DoD originator determines that information is subject to special dissemination limitation specified by paragraph 4-505, DoD 5200.1-R.

STATEMENT X: Distribution authorized to U.S. Government agencies and private individuals of enterprises eligible to obtain export-controlled technical data in accordance with DoD Directive 5230.25; (date). Controlling DoD office is (insert).